Spiritual Life

The Wake-up Call

The Way Back to God

by Mark Zaretti

"Spiritual Life Explained: The Wake-up Call

The Way Back to God"

by Mark Zaretti

Published by The Way Back Group Ltd: https://thewaybackgroup.org

© 2023 The Way Back Group Ltd. All Rights Reserved.

No portion of this book may be reproduced in any form without permission from the publisher, except as permitted by U.K. copyright law. For permissions please contact: info@thewaybackgroup.org

ISBN 979-8866156290

Current Books in *The Way Back* series
by Mark Zaretti:

The Way Back, The Six Virtues:
A Companion Guide (2019)

Spiritual Life Explained: The Wake-up Call
The Way Back to God (2023)

Table of Contents

Preface..1
Part 1: Belief Versus Experience..3
   Chapter 1: The Journey Begins...3
   Chapter 2: Desire for Truth..4
   Chapter 3: Transcending Beliefs..6
   Chapter 4: Spiritual Experience..7
   Chapter 5: Resisting the Idea of "God"......................................10
   Chapter 6: From Within the Stillness...13
   Chapter 7: Pillars of Spiritual Life..14
Part 2: Free Will...16
   Chapter 8: Guided by God..16
   Chapter 9: Head Versus Heart..16
   Chapter 10: When We Do Wrong..18
   Chapter 11: Always a Choice?..19
Part 3: Health and Healing..21
   Chapter 12: Physical Feedback..21
   Chapter 13: Toxic People..23
   Chapter 14: Personal Responsibility..27
   Chapter 15: The (Dark) Secret..28
Part 4: Being Holistic..40
   Chapter 16: Wisely Receptive?...40
   Chapter 17: Bonus Information..44
   Chapter 18: So Why Are We Alive?..54
   Chapter 19: What is "We"?...59
   Chapter 20: Soul Growth..60
   Chapter 21: God's Delight...63
   Chapter 22: Respect Your Higher-Self?.....................................64
   Chapter 23: Orientation..70
   Chapter 24: Living a Good Life...72
   Chapter 25: Is Wealth Important?...76
   Chapter 26: The Wrong Partner..78
   Chapter 27: Meaningful Relationships.......................................79
   Chapter 28: Spiritual, but Asleep..83
   Chapter 29: Fostering the Relationship.....................................84
Epilogue...89
   Chapter 30: Change is Now...91
   Chapter 31: God Bless..93
   Chapter 32: Through Me, Not From Me....................................95
Appendix..99
   Links..99

Preface

Over the years I have learnt that there is a much bigger picture and that the best way to be a positive part of it is to stop trying to be. We are not meant to be striving to make a difference, rather we are meant to be still, neutral, and humble. In this way we rise up from *"Doing what we think we need to do"*, towards *"Being what God intends us to be"*.

I did not plan to write this book, rather it just happened because I was not trying to write this book. In September 2023 I started *"Bringing down"* a deeper understanding of human spiritual nature and as a result, on the 12th September 2023, I recorded a four part mini-podcast series called *"Spiritual Life Explained"*. Although self-contained it naturally followed on from the forty plus episodes I had already produced during the preceding years.

These four podcasts contained higher information, which was faithfully delivered as a scripted monologue. However, the last episode also contained bonus unscripted guidance for all seekers of truth, which was recorded later on in October 2023.

Due to the positive feedback I had received on the impact these podcasts have had upon many good people, I was guided to write this not-for-profit book to share the guidance within these podcasts with a wider audience.

Parts 1 to 3 were pre-scripted and so what you will read below is based almost verbatim on those parts. However when translating what was spoken into written text, sometimes nuances and meanings are lost in the absence of tonality, pacing, and body-language. This is especially the case for the more spontaneous, unscripted elements of Part 4, which truly were a gift that came *through* me, not *from* me.

Therefore what follows is, as much as is possible, a direct record of what was spoken in the podcasts, albeit sympathetically edited to provide more clarity while remaining faithful to the original message. In this way nothing of value is lost when translating the living spoken words into print on the pages of a book. If anything, this book affords me the chance to deepen the message, so that you get even more than was available in the podcasts.

Treat this small book as a journey; do not seek to reach the last page, rather seek the truth behind the words as you go.

God bless you and all who have God in their heart.
Mark P Zaretti.

Part 1: Belief Versus Experience

Chapter 1: The Journey Begins

Over the last few years I have been sharing my spiritual journey with you on this podcast, and it is truly a journey I did not expect. It started when I was about seven, but back then podcasts did not exist and neither did the internet. However, running pretty much on pure intuition and a strong inner-sense, by eighteen I was already seeking.

Like many others, that seeking led me to meditation, which makes sense because if we are looking for answers beyond the physical world around us, then we are likely to end up looking "*Inwards*" rather than "*Outwards*".

I discovered *The Path* of "*Light and Sound Meditation*" and after thousands of hours of practice spanning more than a decade I attained states of awareness that I could not have imagined.

Along the way some spiritual teachers/masters tried hard to convince me and their other students that "*God did not exist*" and that "*Jesus was made up*". But it seems truth will always come out and eventually I found the limits of their teachings and started to comprehend that not all we had been taught was true.

These falsehoods were not just about God and Jesus but also included matters like what happens after we pass away and even down to the source of spiritual light.

It is a negative path to dwell on someone else's wrongdoing, whatever their reasons, and so instead of being bitter and blameful I chose to learn from the experiences and importantly take responsibility for allowing myself to be misled. Having been deceived it made me even more appreciative of the importance of putting truth first, no matter what.

Chapter 2:   Desire for Truth

As my desire for truth grew then many other falsehoods I had picked up started to fall apart and I distanced myself from those who were deliberately being dishonest. I was not alone and other people I knew were starting to *"Wake up"* to the truth too.

So it was about that time that I started producing videos, and in time podcasts, to share what I was discovering with good people like them, and you.

I carried on meditating and even revealed spiritual light and sound energy to a number of people. So over the last decade I have deliberately and consciously put truth first and piece by piece let go of what I was led to believe and I have got to say:

"The truth is far more amazing"

And frankly the truth is far more simple too. So why reflect on the past here? Well I mention it to give context to what I say next. You see when I now talk about things like *"God"*, *"Jesus"*, *"Love"*, or *"Light"*, it is not because *"Someone told me in the past"*, nor *"That's what my teacher said"*. Neither is it that I simply grew up with those ideas from childhood and never questioned them.

Rather it is because I was pushed away from those truths and it is only through the conscious choice to find the truth, even if it was the opposite of what I believed at the time, that I have overcome deception to come to the fact of God, Jesus, Love and Light.

Fact?

You notice I say *"Fact"*, which I know is quite bold. When I was a kid I was taken to church where a priest told me there was Jesus and God and asked me to believe them. I did.

When I was at university studying biology we were indoctrinated into the belief that life is a chemical accident, nothing more, and I went along with it.

When I started advanced light and sound meditation, the master and teachers said there was no such thing as God or Jesus and they made it clear that if I was to get their help I had to believe them. So I did.

It is only when I stopped *"Believing"* and started valuing truth that I discovered that almost everything I had believed, or rather had been encouraged to believe by others like priests, scientists, and spiritual gurus, was wrong. Religion had not really got it right; science is only concerned with the tangible; and the numerous *"Spiritual groups"* seemed at best confused.

Chapter 3: Transcending Beliefs

None of what they claimed matched what I was able to experience within inner-stillness. Now I am not saying I had got it right, but rather, I had stopped valuing belief, whether that was religion, science, or spiritual philosophy, and instead started to really put experience first.

Beliefs can change, but what we know from our own deepest inner-experience, when we are really present and awake, truly transcends belief. But many people never get past ideas and beliefs.

So truth based upon direct personal experience is obviously very important to me, how about you? The journey to seek it is still ongoing and perhaps it is not a journey with a destination, but rather a way of being?

However we view the pursuit of truth though, I truly hope that if you are reading this it is because on some level you appreciate the value of experience over beliefs? Perhaps you have never really thought about it before? If so, take a moment and ask yourself: *"What is more precious to you, what you have picked up from others in your life or what you absolutely know from your own personal experience?"*

Chapter 4: Spiritual Experience

If experience trumps belief for you then you are not alone and perhaps what I am going to share will help you, and those you care about, on your journey to seek the truth. I know that I have been helped by open-minded people along the way too, and that is the point!

This is not about me saying something and you believing it, rather it is about us being mature enough to listen without prejudice and to recognise what is belief and what resonates for you as truth. You can believe in something that is also true, but would you rather know it with a certainty that transcends mere belief?

All this said, seeking the truth, especially spiritual truth, is never going to be a personal journey since there is only one truth. So whoever seeks it will eventually find the same truth as others, since absolute truth must be the same for everyone.

To that end I have made a point of being very open and honest in the podcasts over the years, because this is a journey, and the destination is still ahead of us all. As I have come to understand things from experience you may have heard me say:

"To seek the truth, is to seek God."

You have also probably heard me explain that God does not belong to religion and neither does Jesus, who was, and still is, very real, irrespective of what some would have us believe.

So all this brings us to our more recent podcasts such as:

- ➢ #33: *"How do I Have More God in my Life"*
- ➢ #37: *"Closer to God"*
- ➢ #40: *"I am sorry to tell you that might not be spiritual"*
- ➢ #42: *"Reverence to God"*
- ➢ #43: *"For the Love of God and Jesus"*

Quite a contrast to the first few podcasts on topics like *"Meditation"* and *"How to develop chakra awareness"*, right? Those older topics on meditation seem far away from the more profound realisations and concepts I have shared with you over the last few years, but those older ones were vital steps from there to here, at least for me.

I would like you to be really honest with yourself. Do you find it comfortable to listen to topics like *"Meditation, auras and chakras"*, whereas talking about *"God"* puts you off or makes you feel uneasy? If so then I totally get it and please understand that I was once a bit like that too, just like many others.

Back then even I would have been surprised to learn that my future-self would be talking about *"God and Jesus"*! Back then I was not looking for God, rather I desired truth and this made me overcome my own fears and limiting beliefs.

Chapter 5: Resisting the Idea of "God"

I know from my own experience that like most people who are resistant to the idea of God, it is rooted in some negative experience in the past such as:

- ✗ Being forced to go to church as a child.
- ✗ An overbearing family member or partner forcing their beliefs upon you.
- ✗ People around you making fun of people who spoke from the heart.
- ✗ Indoctrinated into anti-God beliefs.
- ✗ A general fear of ridicule from your peer group.

There may be other reasons but whatever the reason is, it means that most people who are strongly resistant to, or have a strong reaction upon hearing the words *"God"* or *"Jesus"* are living according to a strong belief system, and one that is most often grounded in fear.

It is not necessarily their fault and they may not even be aware of it or understand the reason, it is just how they have learnt to react. Whether you can personally relate to this or not I would like you to contemplate two simple things:

Prejudice

Firstly please listen to these three statements and notice how they make you feel, how you really and honestly react:

*"Behind all that is good is **God**."*

*"**God** is what gives us life."*

*"**God** guides us."*

Now, notice what changes in your reaction when we substitute the word *"God"* for something different?:

*"Behind all that is good is **Love**."*

*"**Love** is what gives us life."*

*"**Love** guides us."*

Now this may seem like a bit of word play fun, but if you reacted negatively to *"God"* compared to your reaction to *"Love"* then it demonstrates that you are responding according to conditioned beliefs.

If you are without prejudiced beliefs then the response would be identical irrespective of the words used. Interesting.

Proof

So secondly, do you realise that:

> *"There is absolutely no physical proof for the existence of God."*

But:

> *"There is absolutely no physical proof that God does not exist."*

Therefore coming from pure logic rather than prejudice, a rational, neutral, and wise person would take the stance of: *"I am open to the possibility that God exists and desire to know the truth by my own experience"*, or words to that effect. How would you phrase it for you?

Interestingly *"Being open to possibility and desiring to know the truth based on personal experience rather than just accepting a belief"*, one way or the other, is a pretty good definition of *"Being spiritual"*.

In order to be rational and inquisitive you need to be consciously present rather than habitual in your thinking and also more receptive to the subtle and non-physical, such as inspiration and intuition, which are amazing qualities for any person to develop, irrespective of the reason why.

So if someone has a negative reaction to the word "*God*", then it could indicate that they are not being logical, rational, or neutral but rather are strongly grounded in an anti-God belief, which for a variety of reasons is most likely motivated by either fear or ego, ultimately derived from other people's ideas.

Chapter 6: From Within the Stillness

Even if this discussion does not relate to you directly it is important to be able to have compassion and understanding of why some people may be strongly polarised in their opinions and at least from me, there is no judgment, since I have been on both sides of the line.

Having put truth first then the more recent podcasts I have produced tell of an unfolding exploration into the nature of our relationship with God and Jesus, in a spiritual, experienced-based, non-religious, non-belief, oriented way.

I started discovering truth from within the stillness of meditation, and though I reached the end of the meditation journey and now no longer meditate, the spiritual journey is still unfolding. How amazing is that! What I originally thought was the goal: *"Enlightenment"*, was just the means to discover something far greater!

Chapter 7: Pillars of Spiritual Life

But now I want to turn our focus back to us, to YOU, and make sense of these higher revelations from the perspective of our everyday lives. So let us explore three topics, which may seem unrelated at first, but which are tightly interwoven and together are three important pillars of a spiritual life. *"What are they?"* They are:

1. Free Will

2. Health and Healing

3. Being Holistic

These topics are not just going to help us to live more gracefully, increasing in spirituality, and becoming closer to God. They are also going to answer some important questions like:

"Why does healing not work for some people?"

"Why manifesting and the Law of Attraction may actually be spiritually counter-productive?"

"Why are some spiritual people struggling so much?"

Once we understand these three pillars better we should find more ease in life. I know that is a pretty big claim, so lets find out how this all unfolds.

From the Heart

Spiritual growth has very little to do with deep intellectual understanding and philosophy, rather it comes from the heart, so lets make it easy for ourselves.

Take a deep breath, and simply intend to be in your heart. Think of it as: *"That's where your spirit is"* and so your heart is the *"Seat of your higher-self"*. Would it be wiser to deliberately include your higher-self?

"More love, less thinking; more being, less doing."

Part 2: Free Will

"Free Will" can be thought of as that special gift a human has to be able to make a choice in any situation. Without Free Will we would be totally habitual and would respond to our environment in a robotic pre-determined way. So it would be prudent to consider: *"Where does choice come from and what is it based upon?"* How is it that in any situation there are at least two options?

Chapter 8: Guided by God

Fundamentally you are always being guided by God to become closer to God. This guidance comes via your spirit, which you could think of in simplistic terms as *"The receiver of God's desire and intention for you to be good"*.

Your spirit then presents you with guidance, which is how in almost all situations, be they seemingly important or trivial, you always know right from wrong; good from bad.

Chapter 9: Head Versus Heart

The good choice is the one that will take you closer to God, and this is the one that came from your spirit. The other choice, or choices, take you in the opposite direction, away from God, and come from your brain, your habits, and perhaps even ego or fear.

This is the archetypal "*Head versus heart*" situation, though the reality is a little more nuanced, but let us keep it simple for now.

So given a choice between what God is guiding you to do (heart) and what your lower-self is presenting as an alternative response (head), then:

"Free Will is your ability to make the wrong decision."

When you think about it, without Free Will then God would guide you, you would react to that guidance, and you would evolve becoming higher in vibration, virtue and goodness; moving closer to God. But it would be almost robotic, a kind of unconscious automated reaction and thus of little real value. By having Free Will then the fact you have to consciously make a good choice means that it has great value when you choose what is good.

This reveals that all that is good in who you are is because you have listened to God and chosen the choices your spirit presented. So those that listen to God become more good, even if they do not consciously know about God.

When God perceives humanity, the people who are really good are the ones who are more receptive to God's guidance. Do you consider yourself a good person? Well have you ever contemplated how you became good?

Before we move on though it is worth understanding that:

"The more you make the right choices, the easier it gets."

In this way, when your lower-self is well aligned with goodness and is spiritually mature, then often it (head) presents the same choice as your spirit (heart) and so there is no sense of choice, you already know what the right thing to do is and you just do it. But you got there by previously making the right choices and so you have grown through experience.

Chapter 10: When We Do Wrong

So what about those times when we have done wrong having made bad choices? Well, for Free Will to work, God does not intervene, rather God totally respects your right to choose, make mistakes, and will remain neutral.

This means that you could in theory turn so far away from God by ignoring God's guidance that you become bad. God wont intervene but that does not mean you are alone. For those who are going the wrong way down the metaphoric path, there is still guidance and this leads onto the next topic: *"Health & Healing"*.

Chapter 11:   Always a Choice?

But before we go more into health and healing to explain why some people just cannot be healed, let us recap. We understand that we have always got a choice in any situation and that at least one choice is the right choice. *"But"*, I hear you say, *"It is not that easy. What about if someone is imposing their will on us?"* or, and this really happens, *"There is negative influences beyond our control?"*.

Well God is always there and there is not anyone, anything, or any force that can push God aside, so God is always there and the right choice, the truthful choice, is always there too. It is our perception that makes the right choice seem out of reach.

And *"Yes"*, sometimes making the right choice is really tough. But your higher-self is there guiding you and it has got the positive experience of every single life you have ever had up till now to draw upon. So if you need courage, fortitude, wisdom, strength, positivity or tolerance for example, you have got it! And if you use these positive qualities, then you actually enrich your higher-self. For example, if you show courage to do what is right, then your higher-self grows in courage because you have demonstrated courage. Then in the future you will have more courage to draw upon.

Doing what is right is a win win situation; you win and your higher-self wins. So at the moment of choice, you have got the guidance from God to do what is right (via your spirit) and you have got the resources and support of your higher-self willing you on to do what is right too.

We can still make the wrong choice for a number of reasons including habit, ego, and fear and so it would be nice if we got even stronger guidance when we are going in the wrong direction. The good news is that you do and you have most likely already experienced it, which leads on to Part 3.

Part 3: Health and Healing

In Part 2 we explored "*Free Will*" and we learnt that all choices are either bringing us closer to God or moving us in the wrong direction, further from God. This is the same whether a person believes in God or not, since God's love and support is always present for all of humanity.

Now if we are going in the wrong direction then the guidance actually becomes easier to notice, but some people may be surprised to learn that such guidance that we are going in the wrong direction in life often manifests in the form of dis-ease, injury, or accident.

Chapter 12:   Physical Feedback

Ever had a bad thought and then walked into a door or bashed your toe on furniture? Been thinking negatively about some worry and then you get stomach ache? Or criticising yourself and then you have got a headache? That is how it works!

There is a lot more to it and rather than go into it here I will simply say there are some very good books on how "*You can heal your life*" and they explain the relationship between ailments and their underlying thoughts in a lot of detail.

Not everything in those books matches what I and others have found from direct experience, but they are definitely pointing in the right direction and a great starting point for you if you are new to all this.

Whether you are new or experienced though I would not worry too much about the minutest details, because it is not about what is written in any book. Your higher-self is not reading a book and saying *"Oh oh, we are thinking bad about ourselves, let me see, page 27... ah, I have to give them a migraine"*.

Your Body Speaks Your Truth
No. It is much more along the lines of:

> *"Your body speaks your truth,*
> *based on your understanding."*

It has to be this way because you are meant to make sense of the feedback your body is giving you. So the key word here is *"Feedback"*. If you are going in the wrong direction, meaning you are not listening to God and your higher-self, then it usually means you are listening to your brain or your ego.

Your ego and your brain are firmly grounded in your physical identity and so since you are now giving way too much attention to your physical body, you manifest the message that you are going in the wrong direction in your physical body. The message is placed where you are looking. It is actually poetically simple and gracefully elegant.

Is it perhaps just that we are so used to thinking that the physical realm is *"Real"* that we compartmentalise and so think that physical problems must have a physical cause and a physical solution? Rather than considering that: *"Perhaps this dis-ease is the result of how I am thinking?"*. But, and this is important:

> *"Not all dis-ease is feedback."*

Chapter 13: Toxic People

There are bad people in the world and *"No"*, you could not tell from looking at them or even how they act. Often bad people are very charismatic and are seen to be doing good in the world.

"Bad", *"Good"*, these are not about appearances or actions, it is about what is in someone's heart or rather, in some cases, what is lacking from their heart.

This is one reason why we teach about *"The Six Virtues"* and how we should strive to be non-judgemental of all people.

> *"How you act and think should be a reflection of what is in your heart, rather than what you think is in the heart of the person in front of you."*

In reality, the majority of people could be considered *"Neutral"*, neither particularly good nor particularly bad, and for them they will lean one way or the other depending on their environmental influences. Your goodness can uplift them.

Black Magic

But if you are spending a lot of time with what you would call *"The bad people"* then they may be affecting your energy and well-being: draining you; bringing you down; psychically or telepathically injuring you with their negative emotions or thoughts.

Most of these bad people are not even consciously aware of doing it and would not even identify as a bad person. There are however those few in the extreme who know what they are doing and are doing bad things on purpose. We could refer to their actions as *"Black magic"* or the *"Dark arts"*, which is when bad people deliberately intend negativity towards others such as magic invocations, spells, hexes, or curses.

This all may seem like the stuff of fantasy and movies but I have worked with people from around the world and what I have found is that this is really happening. It is just that some cultures are more open about it than others and in the West this stuff is not generally discussed.

It is not my intention to spook you but rather to demystify these taboo subjects so you can make choices that support your holistic wellness. Knowing that this is going on means we can fine-tune our awareness and take appropriate action.

So understanding that there are what we could refer to as "*Toxic People*" and that interacting with them can cause illness and misfortune, then it is handy to know that such illness can be healed because it does not belong to you. But it would be less about healing, and more about cleansing you of the negativity from these other people. Your own level of positivity and good intention can also help, as can prayer.

However, here is the kicker that a lot of people might struggle to accept: If you are in the presence of these toxic people, whether that is socially, relationships, career related, or in any aspect of life, then your aura has already picked up on their negativity and your higher-self would have already been telling you to "*Get away from them!*". So at some level you already know they are toxic, but you just have not listened to your higher-self yet.

Have you spotted a pattern? Whether we are ignoring God's guidance and our higher-selves and are therefore manifesting our own dis-ease as feedback, or we are ignoring our higher-self's guidance to avoid toxic people and therefore becoming dis-eased by the negativity in toxic situations, the outcome is the same: *"Dis-ease."*

The cause is also the same: *"We did not listen."* However it is never too late to become receptive to our higher-selves or God, but does it get harder the longer we have been ignoring them or God? Hold on to that question, but for now I hope you have realised why it is that some people just do not respond to healing. It is because the cause of their dis-ease is the fact that they are not listening to their higher-selves and so they cannot be healed as they have not learnt the lesson they need to learn in order to evolve. All the time there is friction between the higher-self and the lower-self, then there is potentially dis-ease. Friction happens when the lower-self ignores the higher-self's guidance.

If the same problems keep popping up then something has not changed, so even if they do heal, it will be temporary and the problem (feedback) will reappear when they make that wrong choice again, often coming back even worse. First it was a sore throat, the next time they lost their voice, then it is something far more life-threatening.

Chapter 14: Personal Responsibility

Right at the start in Part 1 I said: *"I chose to learn from the experiences and importantly take responsibility for allowing myself to be misled"*. The key thing here is for each of us to *"Take personal responsibility"*.

> *"God has not let you down;*
> *God has not abandoned you.*
> *Your higher-self has not let you down;*
> *your higher-self has not abandoned you.*
> *You are not being punished."*

You are simply not being receptive because you think you know best. You are putting your brain, habits, and ego in charge and ending up getting it wrong.

We have all done this. Some people get it right some of the time, others get it wrong most of the time. So be kind to yourself, avoid that negative trap of self-pity or self-criticism. After all you have been guided to this book so you can do something about it.

On some level you are winning already so let us keep up the positive momentum. God is rooting for you; your higher-self is rooting for you; even I am rooting for you, so get on board the *"You are amazing and you deserve positivity"* train.

If you have understood that *"Dis-ease is simply feedback"* and *"You are responsible and thus empowered"*, then you are doing great! In Part 4 we are going to learn how we can build on this momentum and avoid struggling spiritually. But before that, since we have acknowledged that some people get it wrong most of the time, then lets explore why it is that things like *"Manifesting"* and the *"Law of Attraction"* might actually be spiritually counter-productive.

Chapter 15: The (Dark) Secret

Many years ago when I first read books on *"The Law of Attraction"* and started to listen to talks, interviews and videos by the main promoters and authors of that movement, like many people, I was totally hooked into it! I had practiced what they taught about *"Aligning emotionally and energetically with your desires"* and had some pretty interesting results, attracting people and events into my life.

These manifesting *"Successes"* felt empowering and made me want to do more, but it also felt a bit wrong. However it was only years later, once I started to discover more about beings on higher dimensions and the bigger picture of what was actually happening, that my intuition that it was wrong made sense and alarm bells truly rang.

The Teachings of Abraham

If you are not familiar with the Law of Attraction work, it is about deliberately manifesting things or situations in your life and has been brought to the awareness of people on the physical plane by a collective on higher dimensions who are known as "*Abraham*".

The primary person on the 3rd dimension who communicates with them is a lady called Esther and she truly believes what they have taught her and that she is doing good.

This information is all accurate and I have been able to confirm this first-hand on the inside on those higher dimensions. It is through the now famous "*Teachings of Abraham*" that many tens of thousands of people across the world are being guided to practice the "*Art of Manifestation*", the "*Law of Attraction*", and what the hit movie "*The Secret*" was based upon.

It all sounds very positive and people are genuinely transforming their lives, bringing in wealth, attracting partners, creating opportunities and so on.

Abraham describe themselves in their own words as:

> "*A group consciousness from the non-physical dimension.*"

And have also said:

> *"We are that which is at the heart of all religions."*

So that is them basically saying that they are divine, since all religions are supposedly in pursuit of the divine, God.

This notion that they are godly is further suggested by their claim that, again in their own words:

> *"Whenever we* (meaning humanity) *feel moments of great love, exhilaration, pure joy, stoned-out bliss, even the energy of sexual orgasm when we feel that energy flow rushing through our bodies, that is the energy of Source, and that is who Abraham 'is'."*

So they are claiming to be the energy behind all that is good and that they are *"The Source"*, another way of them saying *"They are God"*. Esther also describes them as *"Infinite intelligence"* and again this is a suggestion that they are God since the only thing that is beyond limits and hence infinite is God.

And yet they are *"A collective"*, meaning made of many, not one, and are located on a higher non-physical dimension, meaning they are still located within duality.

The state of enlightenment however is beyond all limits and thus simultaneously transcends and contains all dimensions and so it is possible from within that higher-state to enquire into the nature of anything within Creation, including what Abraham is.

Such an enquiry reveals that this "*Collective*", known as Abraham, is simply a group of non-human beings and they are not aligned with God. They do not have light within them and they are not spiritual guides. I have touched on the topic of groups on higher dimensions who are interested in influencing affairs on Earth in my documentary on Stonehenge: "*Stonehenge: Into the Light.*" [1]

But the important thing here is to recall how I explained earlier that sometimes it is not how people act or appear that matters, rather what is in their hearts. Well this collective are doing a wonderful job of acting and appearing good and benevolent, partly by targeting and working through genuinely good people down here on the physical plane, but they have neither light nor love in their hearts, and their real goal is quite sinister, even if their message appears positive.

Let me provide context for what I am saying as I am sure this may be challenging for a lot of people to hear, especially if in good faith they have invested their time, energy, money and beliefs into the *"Law of Attraction"* movement.

Higher Perspective

God is limitless, beyond form, beyond time, eternal, the absolute Creator, and the one who guides every human via the human spirit.

"There is nothing greater than God."

Therefore God who is omnipotent, omniscient, omnipresent and all-knowing, knows what is best for you, what you need, and because God loves you unconditionally, is always seeking to guide you for your greatest good.

You are always guided by God to what you need, but Free Will means you do not always follow. Life is about you learning through experience and to eventually awaken spiritually and to seek God, the highest purpose of human life; growing in goodness and becoming closer to God over many lifetimes as well as in this lifetime.

The Law of Attraction and other *"Manifesting"* ideologies however mean we decide what we want to manifest or attract in life rather than being guided by God and so we must contemplate: *"Where does knowing what we should desire come from?"*

The Desire to Manifest

It does not come from God nor God's guidance. It does not come from our higher-self either, rather it comes from our lower-self and is rooted in self-criticism and self-judgment of the life we are living.

When our lower-self desires change it is us saying to God and to our higher-selves:

> *"I have judged my life and I do not like the way it is."*
>
> *"I want a partner."*
>
> *"I want wealth."*
>
> *"I want a better career."*
>
> *"I, I, I…"*

Desiring to manifest in life means three things:

1. Firstly, that there is a lack of acceptance, tolerance, or gratitude of the present.

2. Secondly, there is no trust in God.

3. And thirdly, no personal responsibility or appreciation of the fact that where you are now is because of the choices you have already made.

When you proactively attempt to manifest in your life you are basically saying:

"God has got it wrong and so I need to fix my creation".

For example if you do not have a partner, perhaps it is because you are not meant to at this time. Or if you are meant to then you have been ignoring your higher-self who is trying to guide you to the right person who would help you grow spiritually, and whom God has already lined up for you to meet, if only you would follow their guidance you are already being given.

Ego Versus God

But the Law of Attraction and the manifestation ideology means that you decide what is best for you and when it should happen, based on your lower-self's desires. You then try and manifest it through emotional and energetic congruency to your desire.

There is no space in that mindset for God's guidance, because you cannot be saying "*I know what I need*" and at the same time saying "*I want to be receptive to God and my higher-self's guidance*".

The Law of Attraction and active manifesting is all about desire and the power of self, which ultimately starts and ends with ego. It is "*My will be done*" rather than "*God's Will be done*".

The claims of Abraham to be some sort of divine energy, The Source, or infinite means that they appeal to good people who are spiritually seeking. This is deliberate because Abraham's goal, though they would not admit it to people on the 3rd dimension, is to:

> "*Distract genuine spiritual people away from God by taking their spiritual curiosity and redirecting that enthusiasm into seeking personal power, material or emotional gain.*"

Abraham's teachings direct your upwards spiritual-seeking attention back down into the manifest world of desire around you. After all, the more you invest your time and will-power to shape your own life through the Law of Attraction, satisfying your desires, then the more attracted and emotionally tethered you are going to be to your life and its trappings.

The *"Law of Attraction"*, *"Manifesting"*, or *"The Secret"*, whatever you call it, is actually the antithesis of spirituality since real spirituality raises you above worldly desires, relinquishing the ego-centric illusion of being in control to real higher-guidance, which ultimately comes from God.

Abraham are not spiritual, they are materialistic, hedonistic, and dark and that is their real message. But like all who deceive good people they use elements of truth along with good words and deeds to hide their deception and real intent. The Law of Attraction is fundamentally real and can be explained simply as *"You manifest what you give your attention to"*.

However in the case of Abraham's teachings, the manifestation works partly through the power of your own intention, but also because the Abraham Collective actively work on higher dimensions to bring about what you desire on your behalf so that you buy even more into their agenda.

Since God has given you Free Will then God remains neutral and allows you to go in that dark direction and imprison yourself within the manifestation of your own worldly desires.

Abraham know this all too well and so they encourage humans to focus on what their lower-self's wants instead of being humble and receptive to what God wants.

It replaces trust in what is truly divine (God), with trust in lower-self or worse, trust in Abraham, and so you are encouraged to become your own "*Creator*" and thus turn your back on the one real Creator, God. Like so much deception it is sold on positive gains and half-truths.

I do not say this lightly, and I say this as someone who has encountered the collective "*Abraham*" and their superiors many times on higher-dimensions, including when they have gone by other names.

"All that glitters is certainly not gold."

Of course those people who enjoy the teachings of Abraham or who channel and share them with others are oblivious to this higher-truth since they themselves have been deceived and misdirected away from true spirituality. They now have their role as practitioners or agents of Abraham cemented into their personal lower-self-identity. Because such an identity is empowering it can easily lead to ego and so would resist challenge.

Truth Stands Firm

It would be hard for them to accept the truth and I do not have any wish to convince them, or anyone, that what I say is true either. Truth stands firm on its own and does not need defending, rather truth speaks to those who value it when they are ready for it.

Those who do not value truth will not recognise it and it is a fool who tries to force the truth on another, because what you know from personal insight is what you know, but trying to force someone else to know it is lowering yourself into the world of beliefs.

It is wise to remember that everyone who has chosen to follow Abraham has done so of their own Free Will. I was at that crossroads once, just like many other people, and like others I know, we explored it and then realised it was small and a spiritual dead-end, and so left it behind to carry on pushing for the truth. Since God respects Free Will, then so should we.

As with all I share (in my podcasts), maybe it will resonate with people who are ready, speaking to their higher-self even if their lower-self is distracted. And if not?

Well God still loves each and every human and guidance, feedback, and opportunities for spiritual growth will always come to those who are awake. Which brings us on to Part 4 and the reason why so many people are not very awake.

Part 4: Being Holistic

So let us do a really condensed recap:

> *"Belief is the basis of religion.*
> *Whereas spirituality is founded in direct experience.*
> *And the ultimate spiritual goal for human life*
> *is to become closer to God*
> *through experience of the qualities of God*
> *along with humility and reverence towards God."*

God is always guiding you to achieve this and your higher-self is guiding you too. However Free Will means you can ignore this guidance and instead come from habits, ego and fear.

If you go too far in the wrong direction your body manifests dis-ease as a kind of spiritual *"SOS"* to get your attention; literally your body is used as the canvas for your higher-self to leave a message: *"Wake up!"*

Chapter 16:   Wisely Receptive?

So surely the wisest thing would be to make sure we are receptive to God and our higher-self, right? That way we can avoid unnecessary dis-ease but more importantly become closer to God and spiritually mature as a human being.

Well, I would agree with you on that so let me share a really important insight with you, which is something that most people simply do not realise fully.

This life is not the first incarnation that your higher-self has ever had. This life is however a wonderful opportunity for you, and when I say *"You"* I mean *"All that you are"*, an opportunity to grow and evolve spiritually.

But if, for whatever reason, you have been ignoring your higher-self and ultimately God, then two things happen:

God

The first is that God carries on guiding you and loving you. Yes that is right, God is unconditional in God's love and God's support for you. God never abandons you nor turns God's back on you. Your choice having heard that is simple: Be grateful, or take it for granted?

"Being grateful" is the path that brings you closer to God, whereas *"Taking God for granted"* is not. Free Will means you get to decide how you respond and since you have already responded just now, you have experienced Free Will. So this is a nice real-time example of how experience is higher than belief.

You may have had a belief about how you might respond or a belief in the presence of Free Will, but what just happened was a direct experience of how you reacted and therefore of a direct experience of your Free Will.

What was real was your experience of how you actually reacted, gratitude, or taking for granted? Your belief about how you might react was only ever a belief and may have been different from your reaction. This is why experience is more important than belief. Experience reveals truth.

So what is the other thing that happens if we repeatedly ignore our higher-selves and/or God?

Your Higher-Self
Well it is simple. Your higher-self does not have a body, it does not sleep, eat, exercise, or feel things the way you feel things. Its interaction with you is based purely in awareness and if you are not being aware of it, then keeping things simple, it loses interest in being aware of you and the life you are living.

Your higher-self will not "*Go away*" as such, though there are consequences for any person who is deliberately choosing to do wrong! Think of it like this: Your higher-self loves you, values you, and guides you in subtle ways. But if you keep ignoring it then the "*Relationship*" between you (brain, body, and sense of self) and your higher-self, which includes your soul and spirit, is not nurtured and atrophies.

For there to be a strong relationship it requires you to respond positively to your higher-self. This does not mean that you wake up and say "*Good morning higher-self, how are we today?*", although you can if you like.

Rather the ideal response is that when it guides you, you are receptive and you follow the guidance, something you may not be consciously aware of. In fact the relationship is meant to be guidance from the top down, rather than an actual conscious conversation and I am going to explain a bit later how you can foster this relationship.

> *Up till this point you have been reading the scripted monologue recorded on the 12th September 2023. However what you are about to read is the spontaneous, unscripted guidance, recorded on 5th October 2023, which was inserted into the podcast series at this juncture.*

What you've been watching up till now was recorded on the 12th of September 2023. You may notice I look slightly different and that's because today is the 5th of October 2023. I have obviously already recorded Part 1 through to Part 4, so please let me explain why I am interrupting things at this point.

Each week I have been editing and producing each of the parts so it has been an ongoing process which has got me to really focus a lot more on this subject matter. What has happened is that during the weeks of editing Parts 1, 2, 3, and now Part 4, I have realized that through focusing upon these things, I have brought down and learned even more information.

I wish to share this information with you now and have decided that rather than carrying on with Part 4 as it was originally recorded, I am going to stop at this point and introduce this additional information and then we will return back to what was already recorded for Part 4, since that was extremely relevant, and still is.

Chapter 17: Bonus Information

So what you have now is really kind of a "*Bonus section*" and so if you have watched (read) this far "*Well done*", you are getting extra information that you would not have got otherwise.

So we were just discussing what happens when you are not receptive to your higher-self and as I have explained your higher-self loses interest in the life that you are living and therefore withdraws a little bit.

But I need to make it clear that your higher-self has not fallen asleep and it has not gone anywhere. It still cares about you, however it understands "*The bigger picture*" and recognises that you, in this particular incarnation, are not giving it attention and so it will simply stop giving you guidance.

Your higher-self is still being guided by God and it still wants to guide you but it also realizes that since you have gone too far into the world around you and into your lower-self, be that ego, fear or anything else that is negative, then it cannot get through to you. Your higher-self will patiently wait and if the opportunity comes up where you are receptive to its guidance then it will try and steer you back so that you can start up the relationship again.

A Surprising Statistic

Now I would like to share an important statistic with you, if you like. However, before I do I want you to pay attention to how you respond when you receive this information. On the 12th of September 2023, at the time when I recorded Part 4:

> "*Across the whole planet almost every single person was completely asleep to their higher-self.*"

That is quite shocking and includes spiritual people too. Although I say "*Completely*", it must be noted that there were a few people, outliers, who were more awake. However even amongst those spiritual few who you would think would be fully awake to the presence and guidance of their higher-selves, they were not as awake as was their potential. Being honest, I counted myself amongst them too.

Now this mass spiritual insensitivity was partly because of the nature of the world that we are in. There has never been a more stressful, sensory-overloading experience as a human being than there is now.

Sure there have been other times in the past where there have been strifes, wars and similar things, but the world we have found ourselves in is unprecedented in terms of the constant external demands of our attention, which means we have almost no resources left to give real attention inwards.

What this means is that to be truly properly awake to your higher-self is a very, very, very rare thing indeed, and I will be humble and honest enough to say that I had room for improvement as well.

Demonstrating Your Free Will

Now the reason why I asked you to pay attention to how you responded when you first read that statistic, was because your response was you demonstrating your Free Will, and this illustrates just how subtle Free Will is.

People often think Free Will is only about the big decisions. It is not. Free Will is in each moment and can be exercised with any choice you make. So how did you respond to that previous statistic? Did you take that news negatively?

Was your response something like: *"Well how does he know?"*; *"How dare he suggest that!"*; *"I am feeling judged"*; *"I am feeling like I failed"*; or *"He does not know what he is talking about!" et cetera*. Did you take it in any way negatively?

Alternatively did you take that news positively? Was your response along the lines of: "*Wow! Well now that I know that I can do something with that*"; or "*That Spurs me on to be more present and awake to my higher-self*".

On reflection our reaction to that information was most likely either positive or negative, which means you had a choice, even if it was unconscious, as to whether you reacted negatively or positively.

The moment you read the information above, there would have been an internal reaction and your response was your Free Will.

The reason why I bring Free Will up again is because although we have talked a lot about Free Will in Part 2, I wanted to keep it present in your awareness to reinforce just how important your Free Will, and thus the choices you make, is.

Going back to that statistic, it means that to be truly awake is an extremely rare thing, but importantly, it is a possibility for everyone to be much more awake. If you are reading this then you are already moving in the right direction because I am hopefully going to help us all to be even more awake.

Why Are We Asleep?

First though, let us explore why is it that we could be almost completely asleep to our higher-selves, since understanding this may help us overcome it. The reason is simple. Our higher-selves are there guiding us, just as they have always done, but we are often ignoring the guidance.

When I say *"Ignoring"* it is not as if we say to ourselves: "*Oh here comes some guidance and I am choosing to ignore it*", which would suggest a conscious decision to ignore guidance that we are actually aware of.

Rather it is simply that we are not receptive because our focus is mainly directed into our personalities, our bodies, our lives, and the physical realm. So we are more asleep because more of our attention is focused in the wrong direction and we simply do not register the guidance we are receiving.

Most people basically do not even realize that they have got a higher-self, let alone that they are being guided by it. For you personally this ultimately means that whatever is demanding most of your attention in life, whatever the motive or reason, whether it is ambition, pleasure, delight, lust, stress, fear, pride or anything else, it is important to recognise that it distracts your attention away from your higher-self and ultimately away from God. The "*What*" is not so important, rather it is knowing you are distracted that matters.

To understand this in an everyday context take a moment to imagine yourself engrossed in watching a movie, hard at work, playing a computer game, studying, or any other sensory-rich activity. Now take a slow deep breath and observe the contrast as you imagine for example you are deep in meditation, prayer, contemplation, or just sitting in nature.

Notice the contrast between being *"Present within"* verses *"Externally distracted"* and ask yourself *"In which state would I be more receptive to higher-guidance?"*.

So for most people the subtle higher-guidance from God and the higher-self are not part of their everyday conscious existence and therefore they would not even notice if God or their higher-self were not there.

Irrespective of the reason, generally speaking, people on the planet have largely not been giving higher-guidance attention and so collectively have become largely unaware of it. This is how it is possible that we have ended up in a situation where most of the people on the planet were simply not aware; not awake.

Spiritual Awakening

So when I talk about "*Spiritual Awakening*" maybe you can start to understand it in terms of: "*Awakening to your higher-self*" and your spirit is part of your higher-self as is your soul and other things.

You do not need to know what all these parts of your higher-self are in order to benefit from them, after all they have always been there and they predate you. Later we will explore why it is important that they are older than you, but for now it is enough to appreciate that they have always been there for you.

You do not need to know what they are, just as you do not need to know how your physical body functions in order for it to function. It simply functions. Your responsibility is to be aware of your body's needs, like thirst, hunger, and tiredness and to support it, taking care of it and nurturing it. Have you been doing the same for your higher-self though?

So the opportunity before you is to be more consciously aware that you have a higher-self and to nurture the relationship, to take care of that relationship, to value it.

Spiritual awakening can therefore be considered to be *"Awakening to what is already there to guide you back to God"*, which is your higher-self. Your spirit is the focal point of what is already there in terms of *"Spirituality"*.

"So what can help us to awaken?" Before answering this, firstly please understand when I discovered that I was not as awake as I could be my response was positive and this provoked the question: "*How can I be more awake?*", which motivated me to discovering to a lot of the guidance I am going to share with you.

A big part of answering that question was to start to really understand the nature of the relationship between who we are (lower-self) and our higher-selves. Were it not for the discovery of how bad the situation was, there would not have been the drive to learn what can be done about it.

How we Live our Lives

Let us start by acknowledging how we live our lives, speaking generally. We can talk about Maslow's Hierarchy of basic needs, in which we first start with the obvious needs like when you think to yourself: "*I don't want to be hungry*"; "*I want to be warm*", and "*I want to have shelter and be safe*". As these basic survival and comfort needs are satisfied then we go on to more complex things that we do not really need but which we want, like, and desire.

In other words, "*The more we have of what we need, then we start to look at what we want, and then what we like, and so we adorn our lives with possessions and we put value into things that are material or superficial*".

I know that if you are spiritual then for you it is likely that there will be much more balance and harmony in your life, but talking in general terms: As people value material and aesthetic things then they are going in the wrong direction and become outwardly focused so that their time and energy is overly-concerned with how they look, knowledge acquisition, physical health, relationships, and gaining or maintaining wealth.

For most people these superficial things are the fundamental motivations of life, and are often how "*Success*" is measured. We are entrained to observe everything and everyone around us as either "*Something to gain from*" or "*Something to fear*" and so seek to control or manipulate our environment, to move away from what we fear and to have more of what we can gain from. We do this to have the best possible life driven by our health, wealth or relationship desires.

We measure our success by satisfying these desires and so they are a big motivating factor for why things like "*The Secret*", "*Law of Attraction*", and "*Manifesting*" are so attractive. Though as already explained these practices are a massive dead end from a spiritual point of view.

Desire driven living encourages the attitude of "*You are in control and you should whip everything into shape*". You may even have heard people talking about "*Telling the universe what you want*" or

"Tell God what you want", which reveals their underlying egoistic belief that *"Everything is there to serve us, even God!"*.

Chapter 18: So Why Are We Alive?

You came into this incarnation because your higher-self chose to incarnate into this life. It was your higher-self's choice, not yours, and you are not here to tell your higher-self what you need or to boss it around. Rather the truth is:

> *"You are here to serve your higher-self!"*

You are here to help your higher-self! It chose to have this life as you, so that it could learn and experience and grow from you. So you are here to facilitate that, not the other way around. Your higher-self is not there to give you what you want. Neither is it there to arrange for what you think you need or desire now.

Your higher-self really does care though and it is there to help you and it helps you through guiding you. However, we need to get it straight in our heads that we are here because of our higher-selves, to serve our higher-selves.

The Perspective of Time

So a really practical and useful way of getting our head around this is to think in terms of *"Time"*. Consider this: *"What is the longest existing thing?"*. In fact I will give you a clue; it is beyond time. It is God.

> *The philosophically oriented may say something like 'But God is limitless and so cannot be a thing since a thing has an edge' and they would be correct, philosophically. But they would also be missing the point while also proving the fact that God is beyond description and so can never be adequately defined. Any prolonged philosophical debate over the definition of God is ultimately a demonstration of ego, an intellectual battle, to see who can be less wrong, rather than the spiritual pursuit of seeking truth. Those who seek the truth will not trip over the limits of words, but rather sense the wisdom behind them while appreciating all words are limits.*

God

God is eternal; God does not have a beginning; God does not have an end; God has always been and so spans all time and beyond. So the greatest thing from the perspective of time is God. Now consider that God created humanity, which means God created your higher-self! I repeat:

"God created your higher-self."

Higher-Self

Your higher-self has actually been around for every single incarnation it has ever had, including this life that you are living now. In other words, your higher-self is not a fleeting transitory thing, rather from the moment it was created it has had a series of incarnations, usually with rest periods in between. Measured in years then it has been around for a very long time, in fact you could count it in the thousands or tens of thousands of years.

You

You, according to my YouTube demographics, most likely have been around between 30 and 50 years, maybe longer, maybe less. The exact duration does not really matter. What I am giving you is a sense of how you, your higher-self and God compare on the scale of time.

We go from the infinite, the eternal (God); to something that is very old and ancient (higher-self); to something that has maybe about 84 years on the clock, maybe a bit more, maybe a bit less (you).

In other words, in terms of the scale of time we can observe how that which endures is of greater value than that which is transitory. You can think about this demonstrated in your own life too. You might own a pair of jeans for a few years and then they are worn out and you get rid of them. You valued them, but you also understood that because you will live for maybe 80 plus years, then you are more important than a pair of jeans that you have. Obviously value is not only determined by duration but we are using the scale of time as one way to understand something fundamental and so we will keep things simple for now.

This means that some things only last a little while, some things last a lot longer, and God is beyond all time and measure. So when we put it into this perspective of time then we see that at the top is God, then our higher-selves, and then us.

Now the goal here is not to run us into the ground and make us feel worthless, rather to give our lives a greater perspective. In fact I want you to realize how precious you really are.

You are Precious

Now, you may wonder: *"Why would he say that we are precious if he has just said that we are transitory and our higher-self is a thing that endures and has therefore more value?"*

The answer is right in front of us. God created humanity for a purpose and in podcast #42 on *"Reverence"*[2] I hinted at this saying:

> *"Because God intended humanity*
> *so that they could demonstrate goodness.*
> *This is why you could say it pleases God*
> *to see humans demonstrating goodness*
> *towards each other."*

So God had a reason for creating humanity and guided by God, your higher-self chose this specific time and this specific life to incarnate, again for a purpose. So it was valuable enough to God to create humanity and valuable enough for your higher-self to want to incarnate to create you, and so you are the fulfilment of the cascade of God's purpose and your higher-self's purpose.

You, *"Being Human"*, are obviously valuable to God and to your higher-self. You are what God intended; you have great purpose; this life has great purpose!

What I am attempting to do is to help us to orientate towards understanding that our role is to facilitate our higher-self, and our higher-self's role is to fulfil the purpose for which God created it.

Frankly it is quite awe-inspiring to realize that you living this life are directly part of God's plan! But God intended the unfolding of this plan to be orchestrated from God, to your higher-self, to you. In other words, there is a flow of will from the top down and that flow is experienced by you in the form of guidance, love, and compassion from your higher-self and from God.

Chapter 19:   What is "We"?

I have said that effectively *"We"* are here to serve our higher-self so what exactly is the *"We"* that I am referring to? Lets be a bit more specific since I have already mentioned that the higher-self includes the soul and the spirit.

The *"We"* that is here to serve our higher-self, obviously is the physical body, brain, heart, organs and skeletal system and all those parts that make up your physical presence.

But what really matters to your higher-self is your physical brain and the heart. You could say it is *"The head and the heart"* to keep it really simple.

This might surprise you because many spiritual people might think: *"Yes, the heart matters, we can understand that but why the brain?"*. The brain and therefore much of the mental state is often vilified spiritually, with people referring to that part in derogatory ways like saying "The monkey mind" to indicate that the head is often in the way of spirituality.

So to understand why the head has value ask yourself *"What are we here for?"*. We are here so that through our conscious experience of how we choose to react to things in our world, we can help our soul to grow. Without our brain (head) we cannot make choices, whether we are aware of them or not. So it seems that choice and soul growth are entwined and thus the head has real value beyond just the physical and mundane.

Chapter 20: Soul Growth

Our soul has *"Soul qualities"* such as courage, wisdom, resilience, positivity, good judgment and other attributes of good character. Trying situations, which usually have a certain amount of stress or crisis, provide an opportunity for us to demonstrate one or more of these positive attributes.

"The worst situations often bring out the best in people."

For example, you can only sincerely demonstrate courage when facing a situation that is quite challenging and so requires you to have courage in order to do the right thing.

Whenever you make a choice (the head) which is aligned with being good (the heart), then the outcome is that your soul and thus your higher-self grows through that positive experience.

Keeping it really simple, we can observe that it is the head that chooses and the head is also where we hold our attitudes that lead to actions. The head also directs where and how we focus.

However when we are being spiritual then the heart is also involved and there can be harmony between head and heart, rather than a conflict. By contrast when we are in ego then there is conflict and the head dominates.

Being spiritual means we are receptive to our soul and our spirit and, even if unconsciously, we heed their guidance which comes via the heart. This is possible because of humility, which again is to do with the heart. However, we need to actually act upon the guidance, be it in thought or deed, and transforming guidance into action is to do with the head.

So without the capacity to explore thoughts, ideas, and concepts, and act on them then there is no choice. We would simply react automatically and there would be no Free Will. However since we can make a choice, then there is great benefit and value from making positive choices.

So earlier I asked you to pay attention to how you responded when I gave you some information. If your response was positive then it moved you up because you demonstrated wisdom, neutrality, and good judgment, all of which are good qualities of character belonging to the soul and the spirit.

By reacting positively to potentially challenging information your lower-self demonstrated goodness and hence more alignment with God in that moment. That demonstration and the positive outcome will be *"Remembered"* by your soul, becoming a resource to draw and build upon in the future. Your soul will have grown in those good qualities you demonstrated.

If however you went the other way and reacted negatively, you missed the opportunity for soul growth and potentially you grew in ego. But that is okay. Do not give yourself a hard time; do not be critical since to do so would be to pile on even more negativity. Rather intend to be positive next time since another opportunity to demonstrate Free Will will undoubtably come along giving you an opportunity to learn from this. Next time you may choose a more neutral, wise, positive and higher-response.

So you see it is because we have got a brain that we are able to choose and because we have got a heart we are able to come from a stance of love. Again though, you might ask *"But, why do we (lower-self) have value?"* to which I would say:

> *"Because through the positive choices we make*
> *and the resulting experiences we have in this life,*
> *we bring our higher-self closer to God."*

So your higher-self totally loves you and adores you and wants what is best for you. However in the previous part where we discussed how the "*Law of Attraction*" is basically ego-driven and is the antithesis of spirituality, so you may be wondering how you can have what is best for you if it is wrong to desire and to actively try and manifest nice things in life.

The good news is there is actually a natural and harmonious way where you can have nice things in life and enjoy a beautiful life, while living harmoniously with who you are, your higher-self, and God. We will explore this a little later on.

Chapter 21: God's Delight

First I want to share something quite inspiring with you. Whenever you make a choice and you react in a positive way, the goodness is not just what happens in your head and heart as experienced by you down here.

> *"As a human,*
> *every time you demonstrate goodness*
> *it actually pleases God."*

Now I am not going to go into too specific a detail here, I just want you to know that the spark of joy that comes from God when you are good is actually put into your heart!

At the end of your physical life the amount of good that you have done, in other words the amount of joy you have brought God because it pleases God when you are good, goes from your physical heart into your higher-self!

> *"The joy you bring God in this life
> carries on in your higher-self,
> enduring beyond your death."*

That is a truly beautiful thing. Your goodness will literally carry on long after you have gone and the next life that you incarnate into will benefit from it. This is so beautiful and is one of the reasons why I wanted to do this extra recording and interrupt Part 4 so that I could put this extra information in.

Chapter 22: Respect Your Higher-Self?

In the book *"The Six Virtues"* I introduce six different qualities of character that help us to become more good, more godly, and closer to God, and one of them is *"Respect"*.

Each of The Six Virtues can be explored in terms of the stance of:

1. How they relate towards **self**

2. How they relate towards **others**

3. How they relate towards **God**

Now that we are starting to better understand that we are far more than just our lower-self and really have a higher-self too then I would like to expand our appreciation about how we can apply The Six Virtues in relation to ourselves to deliberately include our higher-self. In other words *"Self"* now means *"The lower-self AND the higher-self"*.

> *"You are inseparable from your higher-self.*
> *Stop thinking 'we', start being 'We'."*

We can now look at the virtue of *"Respect"*, which goes hand-in-hand with *"Deference"*, as an example to learn from. True respect/deference basically indicates that there are things or people that we should respect because they are higher or greater.

Ultimately then, that which commands the greatest respect must be God since God is above all. Acknowledging this does not put us down, rather it recognizes the value of what is greater. Therefore we can explore our relationship to God and to our higher-self in different ways.

Earlier we looked at this relationship in terms of *"Time"* demonstrating how time helps us understand why we should respect God and our higher-self, since they have been around much longer. So now I invite you to contemplate your part in this much bigger picture again, but in different ways so that we can grow appropriately in reverence. Lets first explore this in terms of "*Awareness*".

Awareness

Ask yourself: "*What has the most awareness?*" and obviously the answer is "*God*", but have you ever considered God's awareness? Below God, your higher-self is still higher up than you, just as it is much older too. Your higher-self has much more clarity than you because it is not physically limited to the 3rd dimension plane. But by comparison it has far less than God.

Certainly in terms of spiritual awareness, our lower-self on the physical 3rd dimension plane has barely any, if at all. That is why we have to practice sitting in stillness and letting go of the physical just to have any spiritual awareness at all, what some might call meditation, though meditation is not really necessary.

So compared to our physical lower-self our higher-self has vastly more spiritual awareness and beyond that God is great. But as I have stressed before, pointing this out is not done to put us down, rather it is to put the importance and preciousness of this life into perspective.

How amazing is it then when you, the lower-self, has an intention to give your awareness to your higher-self and even more so to God! Since your awareness is so limited, then what an amazing act of respect it is, when you direct your awareness towards what truly matters.

Knowledge

Let us now look at "*Knowledge*" and by now it should be clear how this will unfold. Only God is all knowing but our higher-self, having lived for many incarnations, and having a much higher perspective on things, knows a lot more than we do. Were that not the case then it could not guide us. By comparison what do we have?

We have the knowledge of this life and that is a fantastic thing for two reasons. Firstly your higher-self chose this life and the knowledge you are gaining is a part of that experience. But secondly, as I have talked about, your life-experiences can contribute to your higher-self's growth.

But just as our time in this life is limited, so too is our knowledge about life and so we must recognize the truth that our higher-self has higher and wider knowledge, and greater still is God that is all knowing.

Far from being derogatory towards our lower-self, it is actually pretty amazing to comprehend that God and your higher-self are using their knowledge to guide you!

Before we look at another example I feel I should clarify the word "*Knowledge*". There is a tendency to think that knowledge is the accumulation of information, and certainly many people are socially lorded, especially in academia, for their advanced knowledge about a topic or profession. That information-based-knowledge is great for winning a quiz or impressing people, but it is not the knowledge that has value to your higher-self nor God, neither does it impress them in any way.

What God and your higher-self value is more to do with you having knowledge of what goodness is and the knowledge that comes from being good. It is knowledge from experience, not from philosophy, theory, or study that matters.

For example you will gain information-based-knowledge (head) from reading this book, but that will be of little significance compared to the knowledge you may gain from the experience of putting into practice what you learn from this book and demonstrating goodness (heart).

It is this latter knowledge that I refer to here as being of value for your soul growth. God of course has all knowledge, fact-based and experiential-based, but it is the latter again that pleases God when it is demonstrated by you.

Perception

Only God Can perceive all since God is omnipresent. Our higher-self is still a limit but it can perceive far more than just this life and can perceive the higher realms where it is. I alluded to this in Part 3 when I explained that as an enlightened person my higher-self's awareness can transcend all dimension and have perception within all dimensions, which is how the dark truth of Abraham on higher dimensions was brought to light.

> *"The upper-limit of your higher-self's perception depends on its level of spiritual advancement."*

So what can our lower-selves perceive down here on the 3rd dimension? Well, we perceive with our five senses so we are pretty much only perceptive to the physical realm. Anything beyond that is through sensitivity to our higher-self.

Remember the goal is not demoralise us but rather to bring us into harmonious alignment, prompting the questions: *"Who should we have reverence towards?"*, *"Who should we entrust with guiding us?"*, and *"Should we put our brain, desires, and habits of our lower-self in charge?"*.

We, the lower-self, perceive the least, we have the least awareness, and the least knowledge, so should we be in charge? Our higher-self perceives more, is aware of more, and knows far more. God alone is absolute in all of these things. Therefore would it be wiser to entrust our higher-selves and God with guiding us? It is obvious then that it would be foolish to think that our lower-self should be in control of guiding our lives.

Chapter 23: Orientation

Appreciating all this can really help us orientate our lives as a human being, so that we trust and value our higher-self, and even more so, trust and value God. Therefore we have appropriate reverence for our higher-self and for God.

Knowing what we now understand begs the question *"Why would we not?"* since God and our higher-selves know more, perceive more, and are aware of more.

Knowing that God and your higher-self are there to guide your life surely lifts a lot of the pressure that we put ourselves under. However many people seem to be spiritually disoriented.

Spiritual Disorientation

Knowing the right order of things: God → Higher-self → Lower-self shows just how much ideas like the *"Law of Attraction"* whereby you dictate to the universe what should manifest to make you happy is misguided nonsense that feeds ego.

When people live the opposite of spiritual truth, believing that they are aware enough, know enough, and perceive enough, acting like they are the *"Be all and end all"*, and assuming the right to decide the purpose of their life, then they are demonstrating hubris and ego. They have turned everything upside down and made themselves the god of their life, effectively turning their back on their higher-self and God. They have misunderstood Free Will believing it to be that their will is the will of God. It is not. Their Free Will is the possibility to go against God, which they have.

But such manifesting ideologies that encourage the individual to *"act like a god"* are not the only example in which people become spiritually disoriented.

What about where people put external worldly things like science, religion, gurus, masters, politics, or even technology like A.I. in the driving seat of their lives? Instead of being guided by God and their higher-self from within, they delegate authority and responsibility outwards, away from God, even if it is supposedly about God ergo religion. Then it is the world that guides them and they are no longer receptive to their higher-self and ultimately God.

Now hopefully we have a much better perspective on where we personally fit into the bigger picture of our higher-self's existence and into the biggest picture of God's purpose for us. Furthermore we now understand the natural flow of guidance which is from God, via the higher-self, to us. Spirituality is turning our attention within to receive this guidance and live accordingly. Fascinating!

Chapter 24:   Living a Good Life

Remember in Part 3 we were exploring how the Law of Attraction and the attitude that drives it is really one of ego. So you might naturally be thinking: *"Well, are we allowed to have nice things and situations in our life?"* and as I said before, the answer is *"Yes!"*.

Consider it like this: Above all, you have God and you also have your higher-self between you and God. Then there is you here in the physical plane, and what you are is the experiential vehicle if you like, which means you are here to provide the rich experience from which your higher-self can learn and grow closer to God. It is only possible because your lower-self is fully within duality, which is all about opposites.

Opposition Leads to Learning

So within duality you find lots of opposing qualities like hot and cold; light and dark; yang and yin; male and female; and fast and slow. I am sure you could think of many other examples of diametrically opposed pairs in which one side balances out the other side.

All these various opposites exist in duality and as a human being (within duality) we are meant to have meaningful relationships to facilitate experience and to learn from. Allow me to explain. If for example you want to learn about love then you need to experience love. To have an experience of love requires at least two things: One to love and one to be loved, and of course the opposite is also true, that the giver of love can also be loved.

Similarly if you want to learn about and understand "*Hot*", it is impossible to appreciate the value of heat without the contrast of "*Cold*". Heat only flows when there is something hot and something cold. You experience heat when you walk into a warm house after being outside on a freezing cold day, then you appreciate and value warmth. The opposite is also true; on a baking hot day it is a joy to walk into a cool air-conditioned room to "*Escape the heat*".

Although simple examples, it shows how it is far easier to understand, appreciate and value something when we have a strong contrast to it. Welcome to duality.

We appreciate light because in its absence there is darkness but you need both and this is what duality is all about.

So as a human we are here to become closer to God which, from a soul-perspective means demonstrating the qualities of God, ergo to be more good. Just as light cannot be understood without darkness so too "*Goodness*" cannot be understood without the potential for its opposite.

Duality provides a rich environment within which you as a human can explore being good through making good choices, those that your spirit is guiding you towards. But equally you can make bad choices because of Free Will.

So just as you can learn to value warmth from both its presence (hot) and absence (cold), then you learn about goodness through its presence or absence in your life.

What makes you personally more good is when you willingly choose to be an expression of God's goodness by thinking and doing good (godly). Free Will however means you can also choose the opposite (ungodly). This is why when you are good it is pleasing to God.

You can only learn about and demonstrate goodness because you are in duality, which is the space that provides for the absence or opposite of something. This means that this life provides the chance for you to learn about and experience all that is good including joy, love, peace, courage and so forth. However this can only happen because this life affords you the chance, based on your choices to experience their opposites.

Your good choices are potentially contrasted by the bad choices made by both you and others too. Therefore your goodness, and that of others, stands out against the dualistic contrast of a lack of goodness.

So how does this relate to you having a nice life and nice things in it? The main things that people are focused on when they are doing *"Manifestation work"*, the Law of Attraction, The Secret et cetera usually come down to the pursuit of *"Health, wealth, or relationships"*.

It is not that you are not meant to have health, wealth or relationships, rather it is simply that when you try and dictate the timing, quantity, and the qualities of them through deliberate manifesting work then you are dictating the specifics as desired by your lower-self. This is getting things completely upside down and therefore going against the natural flow.

We have already looked at the connection between health (well-being) and your relationship with your higher-self, so it is no surprise that if you are going in the wrong direction you will have dis-ease in your life. So let us now explore wealth and relationships in more detail.

Chapter 25:   Is Wealth Important?

There is a natural order to Creation, which means everything in its rightful place and everything in balance. Ego is what drives us to go against that natural order. An example is if you seek to have more than you need of something and to desire extremes. This is why the pursuit of unnecessary levels of wealth is never spiritually good and causes problems.

The other thing to understand is that when the ego is running the show then you are far more likely to covet material things to demonstrate status, power, and social standing, and so would seek wealth. Seeking wealth is an indication that ego has taken over. Similarly a person led by ego would put too much emphasis upon cosmetic looks, aesthetics, and other superficial facets of material existence.

By contrast, since duality facilitates all opposites, a person who is more humble and spiritually oriented would not desire these things in the first place and instead would invest their time in seeking change in life that has real value like more harmony, peace, wellbeing, love and so forth.

This does not mean that you should seek to be poor or destitute, as that would be an extreme of poverty. Remember I said to "*Desire extremes*" is driven by ego and there can be as much false identity in intentional poverty as there is in desired wealth. Spiritual maturity is knowing when you have enough and not being led by desire.

Chapter 26:   The Wrong Partner

If you are meant to be in a relationship then your higher-self will guide you into one, but it will be because it facilitates the personal and spiritual growth of both you and your higher-self. It will never be done to simply satisfy your lower-self's desires.

So as we become more aligned with our higher-self and ultimately that means being aligned with God, then everything is in the right order and their guidance leads you into a better life, which might mean having a partner. Or it might not, yet.

God wants what is best for you as does your higher-self. So when you are receptive to their guidance you will receive what is best for you. The more good you become, the more loving you become then the more capacity for love you have, and the more ready for a loving relationship you are, and things will unfold naturally.

However if you are aligned with ego then you will end up trying to dictate the terms of your life. For example you will decide you want a partner and you want it now, and this person should be this tall and have this attitude and these features, looks and so on. But having such a partner might be completely at odds with what your higher-self needs or what God intends for you. You may not be ready either.

But driven by desire people even do vision boards to try and dictate all the parameters and qualities of what it is they trying to attract in life, whether it is a partner, job, car, house or anything else. However in doing so they are getting it all wrong! This is them saying "*My will must be done*".

Remembering Free Will though, the reason why people can and do actively manifest partners and things in life, including via the Law of Attraction is because God and their higher-self do not stop them. If you are doing this manifesting work then your higher-self would have been guiding you to stop, but you did not listen.

The relationships that arise from such manifesting work are unlikely to bring real contentment or spiritual growth since they are the product of your ego and desire rather than the guidance of your higher-self and God.

Chapter 27: Meaningful Relationships

So we are meant to have nice things but these nice things, be it related to relationships or house or whatever they are, are meant to create an environment to positively learn from. You can learn a lot in a relationship and the nature of being human is to be in meaningful relationships because an important part of being human is to experience and demonstrate love.

Life is about the flow of love and the flow of information and ultimately about observing the qualities of what it is to be good through interactions with others.

When you are listening to your higher-self then relationships will happen at the right time according to what you need to grow towards God. So, remember, you are being guided.

What is not well understood perhaps is that the guidance is not along the lines of: *"Go and sit in that bar at this time and you will meet this person and everything will work out"*.

Rather it is very much more about: *"Right, you are now ready for the next step in your life, and that is to have a relationship, a meaningful one"* and so the guidance is to get you ready for that relationship.

In order to understand what it means to be ready for a relationship you might naturally ask: *"So what are relationships about?"* Well kindness, compassion, loving, empathy and all of these qualities of character. So in order to get you *"Ready"* for a good relationship you need to be more compassionate, kind, empathic *et cetera*.

So the guidance from your higher-self will be oriented around bring up events, opportunities, and situations in your life that give you a chance to grow in compassion, tolerance, empathy, kindness, lovingness and so forth.

When you are ready it is not because you desired a relationship but because you are now in that more loving, kind, compassionate, state. Since your state radiates from you then by the path of least resistance and God's synchronicity you will be guided to be in the right place, at the right time, to meet the right kind of person for you, assuming you remain humble and out of ego so that you are receptive to being guided.

So now you have clarity that having a partner it is not about *"You want to meet someone and this is what they should be like and therefore the universe or your higher-self or God should rearrange the fabric of everything to satisfy your desire"*.

Rather, it is about you being aligned with your higher-self and receptive to your higher-self and your higher-self will naturally lead you in a direction of growth that develops more goodness in you and correspondingly more good things in your life: Relationships, health, well-being *et cetera*.

So I just wanted to clarify that: It is not that you are not meant to have lovely things, rather it is that you will be more likely to have them when you are aligned with your higher-self so that you are allowing the unfolding of this wonderful thing called life, guided by your higher-self and receptive to their guidance. Then you will be in the state that is congruent with a lovely rich life.

So the only thing getting in the way of you naturally having a life with more love and joy in it is your lower-self. Anytime you find yourself imposing ideals, timings, expectations, details into to what you want for life, then that is you (lower-self), coming from ego, desire, or fear to impose limits on how you should progress in your life. So yet again, the big message here is:

> *"If you trust your higher-self,*
> *if you trust God,*
> *and if you are more interested in serving them*
> *and being receptive to them,*
> *then you will probably end up in the right place*
> *having a wonderful experience of life."*

That does not mean there will not be challenges, but those challenges are simply opportunities to learn, grow, and to become more good.

So life is wonderful, amazing, and it is just about keeping the orientation right and understanding your part as a lower-self in a much bigger picture.

So we are going to jump back to what I originally recorded on the 12th of September, where we were talking about how people can be asleep to their higher-self, or put another way, at various levels of "*Not aware*" of their higher-selves and hence not receptive to their higher-self's guidance.

Chapter 28: Spiritual, but Asleep

But it may surprise you to learn that even genuinely spiritual people may also fall into this …

> *We now return to the original scripted recording from September 2023:*

… category and the reason is the same.

The moment being "*Spiritual*" becomes a habit, a ritual, a belief system, or an identity then you are no longer present and receptive. Any time you are living from your habits, your beliefs, your lower identity, or ego, even if it is an "*I am spiritual*" identity, then you are focused into your lower-self. Being Holistic means that you are consciously being present, humble, and intentionally receptive to your higher-self and God.

The irony is that the more intellectual a person is; the more they are in their head thinking about being spiritual; philosophising, ruminating, analysing, judging and so forth, then the more asleep they are.

This is because of what I said way back in the introduction:

> *"Spiritual growth has very little to do with deep intellectual understanding and philosophy, rather it comes from the heart."*

Chapter 29: Fostering the Relationship

I said I would discuss how we can foster the relationship between us and our higher-selves and I have already answered that in what has just been quoted. But let us break it down into actionable things.

Being humble

There is a wonderful podcast on *"Humility"* [3] and I will link it below but for now the take-home message is that humility means you stay out of ego, and you are aware you do not *"Know it all"* and therefore you are naturally open to guidance from your higher-self and from God, even if you do not consciously believe in God.

Intentions and Affirmations

> *At this point in the podcast/video I jumped to new footage filmed on the 5th Oct 2023, which as before was unscripted. So again we break away from the formal transcript…*

Intention is so so important because it is how you orientate your lower-self. So if you have the intention to be more aware of your higher-self, you will be! So you could simply intend on the inside something along the lines of:

"My dear higher-self,
I'm sorry that I have not been as receptive to you
but I intend to be more receptive, more aware,
and more present and awake so that I can serve you.
So my dear higher-self I love you, I value you,
and I'm grateful for you and all that you do,
whether I realize it or not.
Thank you, here I am".

Or words to that effect.

It can be much shorter; it could be as deep as you want, but it is about setting a positive intention in a particular direction. Now what is really powerful is to take intention and refine it into an affirmation.

So for example you could affirm something like:

> *"I am receptive to my higher-self,*
> *and I am aware of my higher-self,*
> *and I am here to serve my higher-self."*

It is about you finding your own words but be careful when you are doing affirmations as they have got to be framed in the positive. So never affirm, never state it, in the negative for example: *"I <u>do not want to be asleep</u> to my higher-self"*. Instead always frame it in the positive like: *"I <u>am awake</u> to my higher-self"*.

So keep it positive but also keep it in the present tense so you do not want to say *"I <u>will be</u> more awake to my higher-self"* instead say *"I am more awake to my higher-self"*. *"Will be"* literally means *"In the future"*.

So keep it positive and keep in the present, and that will make your affirmations much more profound and impactful.

So this is wonderful stuff and it is about using your intention or deliberate affirmations to orientate towards the thing that you desire, your higher-self.

Since the highest form of desire is spiritual and thus focused on God then you could take what I have just explained about strengthening your connection to your higher-self and extrapolate it in the direction of God, but as before, find your own words.

Okay we are going to jump back now to what was previously recorded because what I am about to say is, I think very important to hear.

We return to the original scripted recording from 12th September ...

The right time for change is always now, never in the future.

"Now is awake, the future is asleep."

Love

The third way you can foster your relationship to your higher-self is by love. Your higher-self is the only one, other than Jesus and God, who will never leave you, who genuinely always wants what is best for you, who knows you completely and who loves you profoundly. Others come and go in your 3rd dimension existence, but your higher-self is always with you.

Do you love your higher-self? Do you recognise them as your best friend? Do you yearn to be complete? Is it not time you moved your love for your higher-self, self-love, out of the unconsciousness drawer and onto the table of your everyday life. Like having the photo of your lover on your desk!

Be still, take a deep breath, intend to be in your heart, just think one word:

"LOVE"

Let go of the need to experience phenomena or have the moment validated by some feeling or sensation, just sit with yourself, present, awake, and loving.

You know feelings and sensations really are beneath who you truly are. When you are stiller than that emotional noise then you will start to recognise the *"You"* that has always been there, that is ageless, that seems to be wiser and far stiller.

Welcome home. Say hello to your old friend, they have been waiting for you, now take the next steps in life together.

"God bless."

--- The End ---

Epilogue

At this point in Part 4, the last of the podcasts in this mini-series, the audio goes quiet and the video goes blank and a brief message appears saying "The End". However after about 60 seconds of blank screen the listener hears the last few lines of audio rewind and then the video resumes, starting just before the end.

What is then shown was totally unscripted and spontaneous, recorded on the 12th of September. I am genuinely saddened by the state of affairs for humanity, how the world around us has been deliberately manipulated to deceive us about our true nature, and to keep us distracted from God. Having finished the filming the camera was still recording and moved by what had just been recorded I started to speak, quietly, honestly, from the heart about the situation...

Say hello to your old friend, they have been waiting for you, ... now take the next steps in life together.

"God bless."

There is a long pause as I reflected on what had just been said...

That was supposed to be the end of the podcast... *"Fall in love with yourself"*, but I do not mean in a narcissistic way. I mean: *"To know that you have a higher-self and to know that you are worthy."* All this criticizing, judging, *"I am not good enough"*, *"I am being punished"*, or *"it is someone else's fault"*; that is just noise coming out of the lower-self, ego, pride, and fear.

You know most people have never ever experienced stillness. I mean they may have sat still, they may have momentarily been enthralled in something like a movie or music, but that is not stillness.

Stillness is when there is no distraction, when you are present and if people have not experienced stillness there has not been space for them to be receptive to their higher-self, receptive to God.

Furthermore the tragedy is that when some people start to become still, start to awaken, then they get caught up in things like the *"Law of Manifesting"*, the *"Law of Attraction"*, or *"Abraham's Teachings"*. Then instead of them listening to their higher-selves or God, they are listening to some very dark beings on a higher dimension who are trying to distract them from truth and from God.

The antidote or the solution is humility, because when we are humble then we are more receptive to God; we are out of our ego. These dark beings who attract people play on ego by making you feel good; making you feel powerful; making you feel loved, and then you give them your attention.

When we remain humble we do not take the bait of ego, we do not have the hubris of thinking that we know better than God what we need in our lives, *et cetera*. So it really does come down to The Six Virtues [4] and "*Humility*" is the first of them.

So this podcast series has quite a strong message. I have been very open and honest about the history going back in time, about being led astray, but then that is why I value the truth even more.

I have wasted so much time making mistakes, going in the wrong direction, but luckily I remained receptive to God's guidance, and luckily I valued truth. It was putting truth first that got me out of some of the spiritual holes that at times I had started to head into.

I appreciate that my journey is not the same as your journey, nor is my journey going to be the same as other people's journeys. Neither am I saying that my journey is the right way, rather I hope that by sharing these things I help others avoid the same pitfalls and mistakes.

Chapter 30:   Change is Now

Anyway I am just talking freely now and one of the key things I think will probably be missed by most people, was the fact that I said that: "*Change is now*".

There is an idea that because something has been going on a long time it is going to be hard to change. It is only ego and habit that clings to things though, preventing change.

You know once someone has got an identity like "*I am a teacher of Abraham*" or "*I am a manifestor*" or any strong identity really it is only ego that is banging the drum of that identity. The higher-self is not banging the drum, God is not banging the drum, and they have to ask themselves "*Who is greater?*".

So when we choose change, one of the things that we need to let go of is the idea that it is going to take a long time, because it is not. Rather if we are dedicated, earnest, and motivated then change can happen very quickly.

It fundamentally comes down to:

- ➢ Practicing The Six Virtues, but it is important to do it consciously.

- ➢ Taking on board everything that has just been said about your higher-self and God and putting it into practice.

- ➢ Paying attention to feedback (from your higher-self), before it leads to dis-ease.

I have seen people transformed in days, but all they are doing is getting rid of the junk and revealing who they really are. It is sublime, it is natural, and it does not require some spiritual collective on the fourth dimension called *"Abraham"*, or any other name. That dark group have gone by many names.

Anyway, it will be interesting to see how this podcast is received. I do not know if this little chat I am having here will be shared with anyone or deleted.

I did not delete it.

Chapter 31:   God Bless

The last words: "*God bless*". People say that all the time but they do not understand how profound that is. That on some level one human saying to another human "*God bless*".

Well "*God bless you*" is saying:

> "*Dear God please help this person,*
> *please heal this person,*
> *please bring them closer to you,*
> *please do more of what you already do for them.*"

What a gift; what an amazing gift! Did you know you can bless your family? You can bless yourself? You can bless your higher-self and bless other people? God is not limited!

So if you are still listening to this and if I have made it available in some way, "*God bless you*". Really. And if you have any resistance whatsoever to being blessed that is ego…

> *At this point the camera battery died and the recording stopped abruptly. What follows was added on the 5th of October 2023, when I filmed the additional unscripted content…*

You know I deliberated a little bit on whether or not to share that recording with you because it was not planned, it was not part of the script but it was speaking genuinely from the heart, honestly, and openly, and so I have included it.

The camera stopped recording because the battery had gone flat; but I think I'd said all that needed to be said at that point. However I wanted to take this opportunity to thank you, now, genuinely, whoever you are.

Chapter 32:   Through Me, Not From Me

I want to thank you because in the process of recording this series of four podcasts, I had gone back to do more research, which led to this extra bit of filming. As part of that research I listened back to some of the previous podcasts, especially the ones where I talk about Jesus, God, love, reverence, and things like this.

Even though I was the one who created those podcasts, what I was sharing in them came "*Through me*" not "*From me*". So having gone back to them, even though I knew them in great depth, I got new things from them because who I am to today is not who I was when I first recorded them.

Is it the same for you? If you have already listened to some of those older podcasts, who you are right now is not the person that listened to them in the past.

I found that when I went back to earlier podcasts, because there is truth in them then what I get from them now is not dependent on them, rather it is dependent on where I am in my own journey when I listen to them now.

Maybe you have noticed this already? Maybe not? So I want to encourage you to go back to some of the older podcasts and listen to them again because I am genuinely curious what you will get from them and how much you will notice that maybe you did not notice the first time, or the second time.

I think they speak to us at a level that is where we are, so as we grow and evolve then we may get new things from them, or deeper meanings in them, whether they are written, a podcast, a video or some other format.

I do not know when I am going to do the next podcast, I only do it when I have *"The call"* if that makes sense? So I am not asking you to go back and listen to boost the listening figures or anything like that. In fact just download them and then you have got them on your phone *et cetera* so you can enjoy them offline or even watch them again on YouTube [5] or Rumble [6] or whatever.

But it is not about the metrics. I am not doing this work to have a big following or to to get lots of hits, that is not what this work is about. Neither is it for the money as the books are not-for-profit and the videos and podcasts are freely available.

The reason why I wanted to thank you, because I know that if you are still listening you probably get this on some level. You see many people have the opportunity to hear the message. Of them, only a few actually listen, and of them only a tiny few actually get the message.

This is because to understand the message you need to be present, you need to be interested in truth, you need to be spiritually-awakening. And so though many may hear, few actually really listen, and so I am talking to you because you are one of those few.

So I am really grateful because even if you were the only person that benefits from what I have produced here, then that actually is really important. That has great value.

"*Why?*", you may ask…

Because your higher-self will benefit from you benefiting, and God created your higher-self for a purpose, and so if you benefit then it means your higher-self is benefiting, which means ultimately that it serves God's purpose.

So hopefully you have benefited and I just wanted to say "*Thank you*", whether I am talking to one or 100, it is YOU that matters. So hopefully if you have benefited, you would want to share this with others and if you do then I am grateful.

But I am not grateful for me, remember I am here just the same as you; I am here to serve my higher-self and hopefully if I can in some way God too. So when I say "*I am grateful*" I mean that I am grateful on behalf of the higher-selves of those you share this with: "*Thank you*".

Now this really is the end of this mini series, this podcast, this book. God bless you, genuinely.

"God bless you."

Thank you.

Mark

Appendix

Links

There were a number of online resources mentioned in the text above and so below I have provided their corresponding URL links. You can also find these and other free resources by visiting the website: https://thewaybackgroup.org and using the search tool or browsing through the podcasts and articles.

[1] **Documentary:** *"Stonehenge: Into the Light"*

https://thewaybackgroup.org/stonehenge/

[2] **Podcast #42: "Reverence to God"**

https://thewaybackgroup.org/podcast/42-reverence-to-god/

[3] **Podcast #41:** *"Spiritual Strength Through Humility"*

https://thewaybackgroup.org/podcast/41-spiritual-strength-through-humility/

[4] **Web page:** *"The Six Virtues"*

https://thewaybackgroup.org/teaching-and-guidance/the-six-virtues/

[5] **YouTube Channel** *"The Way Back Group"*

https://www.youtube.com/c/TheWayBackGroup

[6] **Rumble Channel** *"The Way Back"*

https://rumble.com/c/TheWayBack